haibun nation
& other states

First published 2024
by Walleah Press
Launceston, Tasmania
walleahpress.com.au

A catalogue record for this book is available
from the National Library of Australia.

ISBN 978-0-6457977-7-0

Design and typesetting by studioether
Cover art 'A Beautiful Aftermath' by J.B. Moran-Dias

haibun nation
& other states

ELIZA
DUNE
DAIZA

Walleah Press

Contents

haibun
nation

Roaming

At the beginning, our fingernails smell of the earth,
the wind ties knots of rebellious strands and all seems
possible. The world, ragged and boundless, seen through
mist-tinted eyes, tastes like a dream. Later may come
thorns, may come eggshells, may fracture and herald
a season of shards. As life gets harder, so may our hearts.
But there, at the start of our journey, still remains
life's elixir—softness of soul, the truths of beauty and
wonder—patiently awaiting reunion, ready to quench
parched lips with its succour.

how I learned to count:
two feet, one path, zero eggshells
pricking a tender sole

In anticipation of fruit

Life is told through mysteries I still cannot fathom,
bearing buds that may never unfold. Why do the juiciest
berries grow in towering trees on phantom limbs?
Is it my homeland if I've never set foot on its soil or
seen its dirt ingrained in my mother's palms?
Is yesterday a lost language best left unsolved?
Why are there so few words to describe the sawtooth
track between bloom and decay? When memories
return to their roots, is it room and shelter they seek?

gold leaf in sun-dust:
the child shades herself beneath
ripe boughs of mango

The flock

In the face of ravenous days, I say, be the long lush calm
across a winter's lake. Abandon the ritual of wanton
preening. Consider the thicket of yellow-bellied feathers,
waxed and parted upon a marshmallow chest, that puffs
so easily on meagre morsels mistaken for eminences.
In the face of a drawn-out close, I say, be the silent
leaving at twilight. Don't fuss or fret when the wind
whispers your name in the darkening light. Simply shed
your down on the flyway out. Don't jostle as you find
position within the season's migration. Be one swan
of many, tranquilly gliding its own grain of air.

arrival and departure
from the vantage of the nest
expends equal energy

One thousand cranes

White origami birds poised above the bedclothes, ready
to usher the malady away. Teal blue gown daubed with
pureed stains. Earlobe crimped against a stack of pillows,
shoulder exposed. The eyelids flicker on-off for hours
batting the pale, silent sentinels away.

Cold coffee left behind on a tray, undrunk. Milk
swirled through like an afterthought, the once-warm
surface shrunken and curled-in from the rim. Now the
visitors, shooed away, return. The dinner trolleys park
outside in the corridors.

From the next room, the bass sound of deep sobbing begins
again; while a woman's voice down the hall sings raucous
hymns and *over the rainbow* ad nauseam. As the light softly
fades and the cranes fly away.

from small or great heights
all petals fall silently
blanketing the soil

Common ground

For the day's rituals, she clothed herself carefully in an
air of grace. Ate the cookies with some delicacy during
the post-cremation service at the cemetery. Forgot the
eulogy her brother said. Met a cousin not seen since
thirteen reminisce in great detail about her parents'
deaths, the still-pain craving centre stage. Head nodding
along in the warm autumn sun. Cold bones now gone
dust. Stale crumbs brushed from corners as a mouth
that smiled too widely snapped back shut. Grief listening,
simmering like an unwatched pot. Blank stares. Burned
wreath. Forgotten favourites. And the ever-rumbling
silence beneath.

one tree has reached bloom
another not yet seasoned
both breathe in sunlight

Left to fall

Evening then becomes the season for these:
unfolding kinks of time; for envelopes and letters
disposed by fire; dwindling kindling; half-singed
mantels and empty bottles, crystal-cut vases snarled
with roots; for vintage anecdotes in fossilised fragments,
preserved from the moment freshly spun;

for draughty piles; frost-etched panes; gradient skies;
a smudge of village; alpine caves and windless grottoes,
hung with glittering glow-worm snares; for morphic
shrines of millipedes and midges, veiled in
bioluminescence; stung by unnatural light;

for the star-sucked, shadowmoon ditch; abandoned
roads; potholes slick with puddles; rotting posts and fence
rattles; for long-gone cattle; floating lungs on still dark
ponds; rainy husks; orchards grazed in compound
patterns, a lament of branches, bent through the
lengthening chill-bone night;

for the alone shriek of a sooty owl; knife-pleat
concertinas; shivering embers; thinned tuft curtains;
an insomniac's dreams of havoc and warmth; for the
promise of company as the clock's hands pall.

soft underfoot—
stirring the damp last leaves
shellacked with rust

A little spider curled up dead
on the bodhisattva's head

He worked from home. His house full of antiques and idols. In the room where he saw his patients, an impressive line of buddhas, jade busts, bodhisattvas and religious artefacts sat displayed on a shelf above the sofa. There the analysand laid for almost an hour at a time and, suitably probed, spun tales of childhood and spoke in low tones about parental defects.

Sometimes the stories troubled even *him*. Why—there were so many dreams of insects, snakes and arachnids, it could make one's skin crawl! It soothed his soul to stroke the cool marble and carved alabaster with the fingers of his mind; while the actual hands filled a pipe, played with his beard thoughtfully, or pushed slipping spectacles to right.

Sunny windowsill:
a stone relic meditates,
reclining in light.
The spinner's spirit
ascends to heaven.

Natural selection

That morning, she was leafing through the Home Guides from which she read: *every fruit begins as a flower, but not every flower becomes fruit.* The presence of a pollinating partner specimen can apparently be controlled. Peaches, so told, are self-fertile. Pollen meets pistil, ovules seed, petals wither and fall away. Weather permitting, this may result in abundant harvests.

The next week, she happened to meet with a bygone friend who had been busily cross-pollinating. Three offspring. Having similar conditions, she was asked if she'd ever considered fruiting. One day? the friend added, with an eyebrow and lilt.

As it was, the something growing had been nipped in the bud many years earlier; a granule not to disclose on chance encounter. Preferred pomes of my own, her words tumbled out. A transfer of anther to stigma in a closed cycle. Pears of juicy barbs and witticism, apples red-ripe with black seeds within, and quince blossoms writ fragrant in the wind.

a good spring
survives all hail-bearing skies
and brings bees

Lead between the lines

Through this tricky time, I have relied on bonsai and
an enchiridion of stoicism. Attention to absence.
Manipulation of miniature details. With the
acknowledgement that happiness has its limits.
Slowly, the insatiability has receded and almost flatlined.
Loss that loses itself, however, has not reappeared.

silence has texture
and a taste all of its own:
the soul's sleeping in

It stretches out to a year. Beyond, in fact. Sometime
soon I will have to skip the dolour and uproot its
shadow. The leaves are snipped crisply and the white,
sticky sap that remains on outstretched fingers will
trap the bugs I have grown to loathe so fondly. Too
frightful, the terms of surrender. So leaden the joy.

conspiring to grow
the bud revives a ritual
long ago forgotten

Hot-wired

Skimming the Otways in a heap no one would miss.
The road prods at the forest, licks along the coast, angling out
like an overbite that gnaws at the sea.

interior air
like a blur
heat hanging heavy

Splinters of small talk prised from burnt lips. Windows all down;
no air con, of course. Tinny lyrics and choruses fling stolen hearts
and stale promises into the salty breeze.

Why stop for beer or ice-cream. Four hours from home. Nine
hours, another New Year. No plans or expectations when the
rain shadow of the mountain's even drier.

leeward, the summer wind
frisks the crook of a back
with idle fingers

Counterfeit

Let's end this by beginning at the turning point.
One thirty-five on the dot, the beguiling was exposed.
How many moments in history have their own official
time-keep? When it's been a long lull between misbehaviours
or random acts of betrayal, forgiveness takes practice
(and it doesn't always happen on the knees).

What to consult except an out-of-print guide book.
A tattered map with treasures stamped by hand on sheafs
specked with black mould. On inspection, the inner pages
flip on pyrite, brazzle, fool's gold. Stitching tugged to test,
with little chance of repair (and let's not forget to
whisper regret at the threshold).

mud pies stuffed in a
pocket when a mountain of
gold was there to give

Hibernation

It seems to wait upon this arrival. A stirring freed of
provenance. Covering sheet, a silhouette *caniformia*.
Pilling skin picked in a handful of regret. It takes
no course. It stales with age. And if it sleeps too long,
a snatch of ruin as it goes under. Damped fur wan
with candle wax it droops, wickless. A cold eye
kept out for dreaming. The other sewn closed.

deceived by hunger
frozen star swallows the sun
(it knows no better)
black cavern, blistered wagon
adrift in Ursa Minor

other
states

Burma

You gave form to me
    yet you are not
my mother—she
came from many lands
none whose shores I have
reached—a breach birth I
was pulled out by the feet
head in the sand
you cannot command
me to love you
    yet the pangs are acute
as you bleed in the rebellious
streets over years of arrested
development—despite diaspora
scattering the family whether
clothed in saffron or longyi I
worry about your fragile future
    yet in giving me up
after birth the reverse
is not true

First day, temple pass

(SIEM REAP)

They arrive.
The tuk-tuks will wait by the roadside.
      Monuments a haze in the distance.
      Children doze in the noon blaze
      by the entrance sucking
dried fruits and candies left hastily
by the hot-and-bothered tourists.

      They converge in one movement—
swarms of hopeful eyes, grasping hands, hands
clasping postcards, hands waving, empty hands
hovering, a blur of clicks and wing beats
      chasing visions, red and gold
      faced glowing like the sun.

Sweat rolls in petalled tongues, salt pools on parched lips
      pressed to part the sea of tiny
      throngs, with girded hips and *no-thankyous.*
They move past the temple gates
not knowing what else to do,
              shuffling along.

Nice (la Belle)

close up
              not the gleam of Mediterranean dreams
        rather a streets-sweep of grime
                loitering on a doorstep
the mat shaken out with a hasty cough
                  under her breath
              she schemes to loosen
        your pockets
her teeth falling out in her fist
                she presses
        a dirty handkerchief for cover
drones
        an elaborate tale
                as lover & I listen to the twisted shrieks
of trams in the distance
                  time coming off its rails

        we are here, but not here

Desolation generation

On the barren Kerguelen
a butterfly evolves wingless to
save being blown to sea. Safe
yet not free she stirs the rest
of the colony marooned in stormy
twilight by the southern Indian
Ocean to follow her
in gritted tracks.
Wearing dusk instead of flight she fights
off winds buffeting the ship-strewn
island (blowing one-hundred-and-fifty-
three between the Roaring Forties and Furious
Fifties) trembling through eternal
night. Anchored naked in the
tundra she's performed a reverse
evolution. A desolate match
that lit the trick (her sacrifice
a stark solution).

A drama without action or words

characters

Crumbling Seawall

Submerged Island

A Bankless Stream

setting

The stage is a dry-bed of sepia, the colour of murk.
A silhouette emerges, a wavy black line on crepe paper;
jagged as an oil slick spreading in veins, thirsty roots sapping
the ground. Crops shrivel between the worn-out boards
the hordes have trodden. Soil drifts away, and whole
winged populations are dissolved to grit. A glacier collapses
downstage. Waters circulate its peak. The curtain falls.
All performances cancelled this week.

In conflict

i.

I read out every other headline
from the paper   (i take after my mother)
— they don't ask but I tell them
I suffer from survivor's guilt—
               but it's not your conflict!

Take in the news like shards
                    lodging my ribcage
all 52 of a single family killed today
— grandfather to grandchildren—
                    (i remember,
        what's black and white
and red all over)

ii.

With head to chest   essentials short
of supply they can't deny
          we are citizens of the world
it's ours to mess up
          unsettled
breath less
          don't you forget it
not the names nor the spirit
          just numbers
lined like ants all wiped
                    out just like

That no rubble of false security
can alter what I collect
are facts
          plain and simple
written over my
          face bathed in hard blue
light browning my pores pixellating
my mole eyes drying out
                    (that were once like hers)
          oh mother

          Another no longer
                    here suspended
between headlines—*now on screens*
inching a way through columns
                    of smoke
so many dead-
          letters burned up
filling gutters   spreads
          with the crushed
entrails of white phosphorous
          remains

In my village

ode to the one million non-floating residents on rare earth

The skies are dyed an unbroken grey.
It's raining money they say. But none have ever seen it.
Forecast for fallen snowflakes that have grown grotesque.
Stamped onto a shrill cold land. Melted to a sickly morass.
I've drunk the once-golden water. Bloated. A belly full.
Watched the paddocks thunder, crushed to weeds of crystalline pink.
While vast, fuming salt plains swirl with stardust and zinc.

In my village no one eats here anymore.
Overturned soil licks its toxic chocolate teeth.
Bares a *grrrrrrrrrrrrr* come-and-get-me grin.
The woods jaundiced. Haunted. Stripped brittle thin.
Forks bearing deep send what's left to the knackers.
Gathering blood and bone for ovens, seared to puffs of pungent plumes.

In my village no one lives here anymore.
Yet toil lumbers on in vacant fields. Metal mouths sow miracle seeds.
Eyes of steel watch closely from their glassy distant towers.
As mountains crumble, they rest indifferent on fluffed-up pillows.
Lying deft in neat, white-washed sheets, they dream of pillage.
Intoxicated in their far-off sleeps.

In my village every aim was made putty under a miry patch of reign.
Decaying statues toppled down with the flood.
Livers choke up waterways with ash and bile.
And sluicers train the wreckage for miles.

In my village rough palms tear through raw silk purses.
Treasures fall through holes in the ground.
Children grub in mounds like worms without eyes.
And the birds turn three times without sound.

In dreams

In Ulaanbaatar
    a child with a wind-up computer
        calculates the deficit of time spent
          on the internet

In Singapore
    a couple shoots selfies on Fantasy Island
        where leisure is a fistful of sand dredged up
          from good-neighbour Cambodia

In Tibet
    a monk disrobes, bites the hand
        of a shanghaied party member leaving
          scripture incised on bone

In Mexico
    a monarch beelines for nectar
        finds legions of loggers
          have got there first

In Suburbia
    a family dive into a bucketful
        of Killed Fried Cut-
        up birds

A mother lode

While I carry you inside
cities crack
with mustard gas
and seeds stay callow
in the sulphur-blue air.
They build fighters
not just larger these days
but faster.
        Left the bodies on a slab
        and drank the milk & cookies
        plucked from the children.
If it were cholera it would be done.
          As I shelter you inside
          bonds are fused
          with soldered steel
          while scarecrows rove in
          used naphthalene suits.
Even bitter fruit was once a flower.
             The world grieves
             for watchdogs on stealth
             from bird's-eye.
             Pamphlets evacuate from high
             drifting through a plague
             of ashen moths
             before they reach
             my duck-billed hands.
I cannot tell a face through its armour.

She said she missed New York too

Bell-bottom trousers till six in the morning
Turkish bath houses turned nightclubs
(a minor trend in architecture)
pencil pines in the Park
hoisted with white strings
of lightning—
originally felled in a sunshower
in the season of '62.
She slurred, 'Jesus, honey, hug me'
(so sensuous her yellow-cake smirk)
then said I should eat more bananas.
There was something lonely
in her every bone
and every elegant heel.
'There is snow and bitter children,'
she guzzled down her beer,
'and golden cabs
with fire-proofing
housing multi-dimensional Star Trek prints
and Goodyear blimps on Broadway
that twist and sing
a rose is a rose is a rose
like Berlin, Irving.'
(American culture is a pop culture)

We passed a three-storey motel
Boy Scout camp
on our way down the map
to our cuttle-fish town.
She was rocking
like a cradle on a bearskin
and the glow was getting dim
when, on the rim of her hand,
was a woodsy landscape.
We couldn't believe our eyes—
six bottles of Tattinger
and strawberry depths of field
exuding the calm of an encyclopaedia.
With gentle nostalgia
we raced down the highway, singing
I Did it my Way
as the rain began to fall on powerlines.
And in the rear-view mirror
not another set
of headlights
could be
seen.

Windflower eyes

why do you laugh
    as the wet apples smack
      tart upon the cold kitchen floor
fresh from your bare gingham palms

     and yesterday i saw you
        wrap an orange in your hair
         i swear it held like Jupiter
against the sun of your face

    yet shown up at a fairground
      some might try and shoot it down
        with their popguns and paper bullets
hapless and coconut shy

    windflowers burn in your incinerator
        eyes, still i feel cold
      when you touch me
and turn to stone

love was buried in your backyard
    in an unmarked grave
     i supervised it myself
from the shadow of the arbour

tell me my attempts are not
        fruitless, tell me your ardour
              means more than what lies
at the core of your brittle candy laughter

   or shall i just eat a peach,
        sing from each to each?
            i warn, i shall don the Prufrock
set fire to your hollyhock

            if you persist to
                  mock this other
      who longs to be
your lover

Mismatched bookends

You and I against the grain
        heading for the end of days
                yet in my head you've caved in.
Blamed the way I read
        these rooms of stolen
                looks and took instead to
reams of books that lie
        more on the floor, the table,
                than occupy the shelf.
While you indulged
        some paperback romance
                by myself, I shaved the sawdust
brushing slivers off your caress
        thumbs on pages licked clean
                of their constant flip and twitch.

Outward I'm flapping mad; inwards, still as pitch.

Unorientable

A polished rice grain
borne in of a melting pot.
Bitter and sour tastes
aren't spurned.
Indian sweets preferred.
Left after grandmother's death
with a smattering of tongue
at age four.

> You think perceived identity
> has anything to do with me?
> Thrown off
> the axis of symmetry
> I choose to embrace chirality
> not map in line with
> your mirror's contours.

Bowerbird
I collect blood and ethnicities
keep them guessing
to the true nature of me.

> *For is it not enough*
> *to just show up*
> *and speak in Love?*

The unknot

also known as the trivial knot
rope's closed loop
deformable circle
universal joints connect with
endpoints which cannot be undone
   with no discernible genesis
   a stuck unknot
   can not be reconfigured
   till formally named the
   unknotting problem
      first, loosen the lariat
      do not resuscitate
      examine the helix
      the longer the piece the more
      we're prone to untangle that
      which we find inconsequential
      which once designated
      cannot be undone
      and must become
      more complex
      before it gets more simple

entangling ceremony

the threads shuttle between us
each replete in their own mysterious knowing:

enchantment unfolds upon the thresholds
and horizons of intersect & overlap

a place to unpack the commonplace
of heart's space, and listen

to the gentle pluck of possibility
                    reverberate

breath is the spirit

is its apparatus to whisk one away
to a place near the after-death
when lungs become a pair of not-needed
a set of vestigial wings to pan the plateau
or hands lost in prayer pressing heart line to head
bred to honeycomb an Everest of emotion
spirit remains blessed as a colony that hums
with sweet citrine candy
as the bonfire melts the valley snow
filling dark crevasses below
with an everlasting peace

a field of emptiness

a broken wing marks its radius in the wind
    when seen from above everything is silence
        the branch seeking balance or prayer wheel on its axis

weatherboarding's flayed from swallowing the gale
    tiny cracks turn the walls a deeper vellum pale
        splintered and brushed in hundred-year ribbons

        time softly seeps through a sweet deadened hush
    saffron robes frayed with the coming of rust
harbinger of peace and mind's eternal stillness

before we're all just dust

are we all just poured   are we all just mimes
from the same ink   to the same tune
some watered down   in valves of rhythm
some full strength   or hushed rhymes
condensed or swelled   that time edits
with first breath   to void life
our fate   that latently
in *kalpa*   discovers
from destruction   all meaning
to creation not   in no-thing
one drop spilt   recurring

what we utter must

wooden dolls

as they sleep
an ache nestles within
stop creaking
one tells the other
nursing a splintered wound
one curls into the other's darkness
clinging to sleep

clinging to sleep
one curls into the other's darkness
nursing a splintered wound
one tells the other
stop creaking
an ache nestles within
as they sleep

beneath the mound

listen

       there are some birds
       who only cry in the dark
       black ash feathers, mesh of beaks
       a gearing of incurable sounds

       long, deep shadows trill without waver
       beckoning me to go down
           down beneath the earth
              where crayfish mate
                 a wolfhound prowls

i swear it is the loneliest sound

       cry of a breeze dressing the embers
       the scrawl of fingers breaking the surface
       beneath the mound

the mind is a buried child

the mind is a buried
child clawing the womb
a sea crab as it scuffles to shore
no shelter when the gulls swoop

       dusk salted feathers
       packed to the lungs
       gush forth a babble
       of sputum and foam
       (an episode reaching close)

we sat in soft moments
my mother and i, separate
ends of a combustible
family line

       a life doesn't come with storm
       warnings, she said
words inscrutably lucid
they stole my breath,
       whether swamped or swim
       afloat with an eye to the sky,
       we all have to swallow
       the brine sometime

she gleaned a small
out-of-place boy
in her dim hospice room

with a smooth chestnut head
two beady eyes
at the foot of the bed
he loitered
flexing his toes
in her slippers

what was he doing?
        clawing, she sighed
        savouring peppermints and chocolate
        circling his gums,
        making sure the ward nurse
        was always on the run

so he's a trickster,
i half-asked her —
clearly she spied him
by the sidelong of her wits
tucked between the
deepening shadows
(an episode ready to close)

        i want to see the sea
        — emphatically —
        eat chips and fish?
        her last, almost a plea

but what could i do from here
drowning in an empty bath
at the end of the line
voice growing fainter
the plug suspended
as it drained out the water

      no tears would come
      that would be for later

the mind is a buried child, a grown
upended daughter

this is not an exit

this is not a dream—
you are screaming
at a stone without tongue
that gravels as trembling thunder comes
transmuting calcite, mineral, bone
yet never arriving to shatter
the ear drums

this is not a gift—
you are distancing
from a fire without flint
that peters as primal judgement comes
grappling space, wind, grit
yet never striving to capture
the last sun

this is not an exit
you are open to—

Death has a short memory

Came by here last leaves fall.
Arrival unannounced. Biker's beard.
Back again. For more. But worse.
Full metal holster. Revving intent.
Offering spectators some gory delights
& rattling sounds like oil-starved engines out of tune.
If looks could kill, Death's flesh would be all wound.
Flash-flood blood. Rotation of spare parts. Cold hearts.
Hell, we're not in the driver's seat no more.
And the leaves will be compost soon.
Swept away like an eyelash from a
once-sweet frigid cheek.
Exhaust fumes.
Too soon.

dandelion fuse

you hit the roof she smack on tile
your nectar honey golden child
youre not her dad her ma confessed
she wish the moon was your address
too man to talk pent up inside
she never cry her eye just dried
gone dark blood felled ignite reply
no grown but blown one dandelion face south
you drone mind snuff her lullaby
out

singularity

beauty knows her own gravity:
her multi-orbit elliptic
strung with equidistant stones
casts a quantum necklace
from just-me to thee
bearing *home*

dear lunula

i heart
your crescents
close d in
you form   a seed
a tear   drop
stalked   unchecked
remains wet
side wiped
as if
in el lip sis
my words
page   smeared
thoughts
un answered
echoes   to you

silence   like sex
a par oxysm
an inter lude
at least figurative
of one

i have stamped
myself   on this page
just   as a child
i   im printed
my   shadow
on paving red
by chilling
pools   too-blue

my body   now
feels old
un stirred
not   in cold
water   but
rolling defying gravity i n e r t i a
making cruel   electricity
in temperate depths
to slide   between y o u

there is   a kiss
that follow s

(x)

i discover you

without weight
　in my bed
　of full
　　warm night
　　fingers of sheets
　　strumming
riffs of rain
　a torpid smile
widening
　on your sex
　　　　space
　becoming
　　smaller
　　　held within
　　　　a glass
　　　on the way-
　　　　　side table

　　　　　the moon
　　passing over
　　　your shoulder
　　　　in half-light
　　　　conducts a seance
　　　　　with the wind
sapling
　　　without sound
　　　　　poised
like a child
　i found
　you

atonal

sleeping
      an edge
  salt
the lovemaking
  a grazing
niched   we seek
     surrender-of-
           -sharp-doubt
 a metric
      possession of this
     no-rhyme
  relationship

familia

familiar is not ease
twisting words
glean into me
thrown scree
off course
a javelin pierces the breeze
lands neither up nor down
just flipped
a map
with no true north
wing strike
to light
too dark
ash greasy trap

ease is not familiar

tanka

spider,

stake
your
death-

defying territory

the familial web

as your life hangs   by a threa d

so i'm su sp e n ded   from mine

cloud shaping

lost deep in Solitude
Park
vast impressions
coax
mellow pomes
mushrooming
beautiful fruit
mysteriously wronged
sadness-shapen prescience
the future enters
us
there is nothing
to resemble
courage
midst the
mare's-tails
& drifting scuds

she sulked alone among the clouds

after JEAN-DOMINIQUE BAUBY

we reached   *point-blank*

                (*enough*)

          a
        dense
       mountain

     the   s   er   pe   nt 's   s p *ell*

    a *detour*
       of   m ira c l es

in   case

         fevered   waters mingled   with the
                         P a st

     str u c k
      we sat   s w o l l e n

    a dog-ea red
        m o r n i ng

     pass i on

      masked

Cold Monday

Today is coiling cirrus
crush bleached pleat hibiscus
two magpies edge the hewn-stone labyrinth
the weather over this valley has changed

Trudging double socks soled grips
sliding grassy treeless cliffs
the sky a bottomless grey

Juiced berry stained pockets
cracked lips empty mouthed
spored westerly's winding southward
the forget-me-nots ruffled in a spray

Neglect garden weeds stacked mound
worms tug beetles gone to ground
will you leave this cold Monday?

Sea of swaying grasses

Morning's steadily warming
while a stream flows cool
from her mother's room
devising its own private climate

She navigates the dwelling
on a little wooden raft
father carelessly marooned
in a sea of swaying grasses

Clinging to the sun-scorched pane
abandoned cocoon glints
hard like a diamond
upon the crusted frame

She blows the massing ants away
summoning a gale to sling
the scarlet butterflies and
wilted birds of paradise
skyward in the dust-caked
light to heaven

The absent gardener

At the bottom of the yard, close to the
neighbour's garage, you planted the pomelo tree.
As we battled off our teens, the tree grew much
faster and bloomed far sweeter tended so lovingly.
You sowed seasons of bloated marrows, tethered
boughs of tumid lemons that bowed and scraped
the dirt, staking vines of bitter gourd, gathering
handfuls of pennywort for your elaborate stew.
As your hands grew harder and your back
wracked brittle, one by one we left you
fending banks of sprawling weeds
and neglected eaves of peat
in your shrunken, arid
garden.

The moon, the soil and the seed

the seed may collapse in cinders one falling night
       husked ovuled shells slip earthbound to the grass
to feed life back to soil in morning's light

bonfire the belly burning bright
       grasp carbon's own as if each breath our very last
the seed may collapse in cinders one falling night

this wrangled lamp weaves blaze beyond its sight
       thrown star-sprung purls engorge all which it tasks
to feed life back to soil in morning's light

garden's scapes spell velvet moss-strewn flights
       as wayward, whooping verdance dazzled basks
the seed may collapse in cinders one falling night

so tend the tessellated orb as a moth might
       adore the surface quaked and cracked in clasp
to feed life back to soil in morning's light

for evening buds this bloom of tenderest white
       will greet new day is what each winged-thing asks
yet the seed may collapse in cinders one falling night
       to feed life back to soil in morning's light

C is for conquer

An innocent green nut slept in wholesome
embrace awoken by budding cells. A horse chestnut,
it grew from winter's dark depths in slow
tiny bursts. Invisible to the eye at first,

it hid itself well. Like a weevil in cereal,
holding strange untold secrets, camouflaged in
a timorous shell. At this stage just a *none-er*,
but being born a chancer it was vivid

and eager to swell. Soon formed
the desire to uproot from its branches and *conk*
a lone bird on the bough. So it plugged up her song,
emptied of lungs, till there was no wilding anymore.

Growth in all, for cordite or kind
stakes its time.

ten lessons from trees

1

nocturnal study:
riverine forest
underground spurs
stunted specimen
no shadows
estuary flats
copse-blackness
former habitat
for gulls, godwits, marsh birds

2

woodland, early morn:
notes, pencils down
greet at trunk level
clasp fingers at nodes
pray, eat air together
(shaking the nests
from our hair)

3

map ancient tracery:
twig to the reason
& beauty of each
wood's filigree

4
annual hex: fire season
resin, seed pod, bloodwood sap
grow-back

5
(there is no problem with tree
if tree has problem
it is *we*)

6
lean to the beech
florets borne unisex

7
make your self a home
invite recycling from:
wind
rain
soil
scat
web
pest
death
thyself

8

nourish networks & shoots

9

look up often

10

take root

November

November is a
cello with its strings knotted
(soundless) in a bow

November is my
heart on slow, mind composing
psalms with the shadows

November is ache
a forgiveness that won't take
your clock ticking low

November is a strand of silvering hair
on this shrunken cloak of recurring sorrow

left with just the stones in her pockets

'to look behind at the emptying air' – CAROL ANN DUFFY

63

just what quiet paths wither sunless to
uncover that lost in shade, just look
at the spell the meadowed river weaves behind
itself, just a slither that tones from inky black at
vivid depths to crimped wavelets of icing greyed, just the
serpentine's skirts fluted in zephyr's wane, just a pair of emptying
lungs in exquisite lonely, just her stony fingers dragging the air…

under lock

'Great wings of butterflies
Streams of shining mist
Wing shields
Over the uttermost woe'

— JEAN WAHL

abyssal   sound   rumbles deep   in lack of
  the left heed   canal   quick silver river   slicing
moss   eroding rock   tossing trout into the air
      gravity's loss   not caught again   too broke
                              outside

              is stillness
                  /
      ears ring-in silence
            seed puts its head
            above ground
      all things meet
          the sky

The end

Pushed away by the fear in your eyes, I decided
to lie to bring you closer again. A greater daring
than I imagined, yet you stayed and played
along, I guess. Every other night I purged
my conscience on rum, cake and fin de siècle
movements. The combination impeccable. I hid
the *sloppy*. You revealed a sanctity that youth seldom
possess. I grew old. You kept board and lodgings
somewhere else. Till one day you vanished
between the seams, to leave another crease
scored unto this mirror. Undoing the knots of
your hair—elsewhere—while I hit zero. Under
the fluoro, wondering how to start again. Meeting
the end.

epilogue

full moon rains
        snuffing the hazed lanterns
            dressed by moths

                    tethered deep
                down oceans of blankets
                    dead asleep

                midnight tides
            the child's nocturnal frights
                realised

            risen light
        parting the dark currents
                    snaking off

Eliza Dune Daiza is a writer and designer of Burmese, Shan, Karen and European descent. She grew up in Boorloo/Perth and the Wheatbelt, and spent a formative period in Japan before eventually settling in Naarm/ Melbourne. Her poetry has appeared in a range of literary journals, and anthologies by Fremantle Press and Spinifex Press. Eliza holds a Master of Screenwriting and has received recognition and awards for performance writing and book design. *Haibun Nation & Other States* is her first collection of poems.

With thanks to the editors and judges
who selected the following poems for
print publication and commendation:

she sulked alone among the clouds
[*Tokyo Poetry Journal* Vol.15 2024]

tanka as *tanka 13*
[*Tokyo Poetry Journal* Vol.15 2024]

epilogue as *(re)verse postlude*
[*Tokyo Poetry Journal* Vol.15 2024]

Common ground [*StylusLit* Vol.16 2024]

Burma [*Meanjin* Autumn 2024]

The flock [*Meanjin* Autumn 2023]

One thousand cranes [shortlisted for the
Dorothy Porter Award for Poetry 2022]

Notes

The title 'she sulked alone among the clouds'
condenses a line from Jean-Dominique Bauby's
The Diving Bell and the Butterfly, Vintage 1997.

Golden shovel homage to Carol Ann Duffy's
'Echo', from *The Bees*, Picador 2011.

Jean Wahl, 'The Word is Graven', translated by
Samuel Beckett, from *Collected Poems* 2012.

Jean Rhys, from *Smile Please*, Penguin 1979.

www.ingramcontent.com/pod-product-compliance
Lightning Source LLC
Chambersburg PA
CBHW042033120726
47911CB00026B/731